To

_____

From

_____

Little Book
DEVOTIONS
31 DAILY DEVOTIONALS

Patience

Little Book
DEVOTIONS

Patience

The quoted ideas expressed in this book (but not scripture verses) are not, in all cases, exact quotations, as some have been edited for clarity and brevity. In all cases, the author has attempted to maintain the speaker's original intent. In some cases, quoted material for this book was obtained from secondary sources, primarily print media. While every effort was made to ensure the accuracy of these sources, the accuracy cannot be guaranteed. For additions, deletions, corrections or clarifications in future editions of this text, please write BIRGHTON BOOKS.

Printed in the United States of America
Cover Design: Kim Russel, Wahoo Designs
Page Layout: Bart Dawson

1 2 3 4 5 6 7 8 9 10 • 02 03 04 05 06 07 08 09 10

For All of God's Children

Table of Contents

A Message to Parents

Perhaps your child's library is already overflowing with brightly colored children's books. If so, congratulations: you're a thoughtful parent who understands the importance of reading to young children.

This little book is an important addition to your child's library. It is intended to be read *by* Christian parents *to* their young children. The text contains 31 brief chapters, one for each day of the month. Each chapter contains a Bible verse, a brief story lesson, tips for kids and parents, and a prayer. Every chapter examines a different aspect of an important Biblical theme: patience.

For the next 31 days, try this experiment: read one chapter each night to your child, and then spend a few more moments talking about the chapter's meaning. By the end of the month, you will have had 31 different opportunities to share God's wisdom with your son or daughter, and that's a very good thing.

If you have been touched by God's love and His grace, then you know the joy that He has brought into your own life. Now it's your turn to share His message with the boy or girl whom He has entrusted to your care. Happy reading! And may God richly bless you and your family now and forever.

Patience

Patience and
the Golden Rule

Do for other people the same things
you want them to do for you.

❋ ❋ ❋

Matthew 7:12 ICB

Jesus gave us a Golden Rule for living: He said that we should treat other people in the same way that *we* want to be treated. And because we want other people to be patient with us, we, in turn, must be patient with them.

Being patient with other people means treating them with kindness, respect, and understanding. It means waiting our turn when we're standing in line and forgiving our friends when they've done something we don't like. Sometimes, it's hard to be patient, but we've got to do our best. And when we do, we're following the Golden Rule—God's rule for how to treat others—and everybody wins!

What's good for you is good for them, too: If you want others to be patient with you, then you should treat them in the same way. That's the Golden Rule and it should be *your* rule, too!

WOW

Do all the good you can, however you can, as long as you can.

John Wesley

Patience starts with you! Kids imitate their parents, so act accordingly! The best way for your child to learn to be patient is by example . . . *your* example!

Dear Lord,
make me a patient person and
let me be a person who observes
the Golden Rule. Let me be
understanding and kind, and let
me be quick to forgive others,
just as You have forgiven me.

Amen

2

Waiting Your Turn

When you do things, do not let selfishness or pride be your guide. Be humble and give more honor to others than to yourselves.

❀ ❀ ❀

Philippians 2:3 ICB

When we're standing in line or waiting for our turn, it's tempting to scream, "Me first!" It's tempting, but it's the wrong thing to do! The Bible tells us that we shouldn't push ahead of other people; instead, we should do the right thing—*and* the polite thing—by saying, "You first!"

Sometimes, waiting your turn can be hard, especially if you're excited or in a hurry. But even then, waiting patiently is the right thing to do. Why? Because parents say so, teachers say so, and, most importantly, God says so!

The next time you're standing in line, don't try to push ahead of your neighbors. After all, if you don't want other people breaking in front of you, then you shouldn't break in front of them!

WOW

When you extend hospitality to others, you're not trying to impress people; you're trying to reflect God to them.

Max Lucado

When it comes to courteous behavior, you're the most important role model: so pay careful attention to the way that you treat other people, especially those who are *not* in a position to help you. For further instructions, read Matthew 25:40.

Dear Lord,
let me be thoughtful and
courteous. Let me treat other
people with patience and respect.
And, let the things that I say and
do show my family and friends
that I love them . . . and You.

Amen

Let's Be Patient 3

Patience is better than strength.

Proverbs 16:32 ICB

The Book of Proverbs tells us that patience is a *very* good thing. But for most of us, patience can also be a very *hard* thing. After all, we have many things that we want, and we want them NOW! But the Bible tells us that we must learn to wait patiently for the things that God has in store for us.

Are you having trouble being patient? If so, remember that patience takes practice, and lots of it, so keep trying. And if you make a mistake, don't be too upset. After all, if you're going to be a *really* patient person, you shouldn't just be patient with others; you should also be patient *with yourself*.

Take a deep breath, a *very* deep breath: if you think you're about to say or do something you'll regret later, slow down and take a deep breath, or two deep breaths, or ten, or . . . well, you get the point.

WOW

If only we could be as patient with other people as God is with us!

Jim Gallery

Talk it over: if your child has done something that is impulsive, discourteous, or dangerous, your natural response will be anger. But as soon as you calm down, help your child learn from the experience by talking about the behavior, its motivations, and its consequences.

Dear Lord,
when I am not patient, remind me
that it's better to stop and think
things through than it is to rush
ahead without thinking. Make me
a patient person, Lord, and
fill me with consideration for
others *and* love for You.

Amen

It's Up 4 to You ...

We must not become tired of doing good.
We will receive our harvest of eternal life
at the right time. We must not give up!

✱ ✱ ✱

Galatians 6:9 ICB

Nobody can be patient *for you.* You've got to be patient *for yourself.* Certainly your parents can *teach* you about patience, but when it comes to controlling your temper, nobody can control it for you; you've got to control it yourself.

In the Book of Galatians, Paul writes, "We must not tire of doing good." And that's an important lesson: even when we're tired or frustrated, we must do our best to do the right thing.

So the next time you're tempted to lose your temper, stop for a moment and remember that when it comes to good deeds and good behavior, it's up to you.

KiD TiP

It's easy to blame others when you get into trouble . . . but it's wrong. Instead of trying to blame other people for your own misbehavior, take responsibility . . . and learn from your mistakes!

WOW

Don't worry about what you do not understand. Worry about what you do understand in the Bible but do not live by.

Corrie ten Boom

Parent Tip

Excuses, excuses, excuses: As parents of young children, we hear lots and lots of excuses, some of which are valid, but many of which are not. It's our job to determine the difference between valid excuses and imaginary ones, and then to help our children understand the difference between the two.

31

Dear Lord,
there is a right way and a wrong
way to behave. Let me remember
that it's my job to behave myself
and to be the kind of Christian
that I know You want me
to be . . . today and always.

Amen

Not So Fast!

5

Wait for the Lord's help. Be strong and brave and wait for the Lord's help.

✸ ✸ ✸

Psalm 27:14 ICB

Sometimes, the hardest thing to do is to wait. This is especially true when we're in a hurry and when we want things to happen *now*, if not sooner! But God's plan does not always happen in the way that we would like *or* at the time of our own choosing. Still, God always knows best.

Sometimes, even though we may want something *very* badly, we must still be patient and wait for the right time to get it. And the right time, of course, is determined by God, not by us.

Trust God? You bet! One of the most important lessons that you can ever learn is to trust God for *everything*, and that includes the time when bad things will happen in your life.

WOW
God has a designated time when his promise will be fulfilled and the prayer will be answered.
Jim Cymbala

Faith in God is contagious, and when it comes to your child's spiritual journey, no one's faith is more contagious than yours! Act, pray, praise, and trust God with the certain knowledge that your child is watching . . . carefully!

Dear Lord,
Your timing may not always be
the timing that I would choose,
but Your timing is always right
for me. You are my Father, and
You have a plan for my life that
is bigger than I can imagine.
When I am impatient, remind me
You are never early or late. You
are always on time, Lord, so let
me trust in You . . . always.

Amen

Saying the Right Thing at the Right Time

6

The right word spoken at the right time is as beautiful as gold apples in a silver bowl.

✸✸✸

Proverbs 25:11 ICB

Sometimes, it's easier to say the wrong thing than it is to say the right thing—especially if we're in a hurry to blurt out the first words that come into our heads. But, if we are patient and if we choose our words carefully, we can help other people feel better, and that's exactly what God wants us to do.

The Book of Proverbs tells us that *the right words*, spoken *at the right time*, can be wonderful gifts to our families and to our friends. That's why we should think about the things that we say *before* we say them, not after. When we do, our words make the world a better place, and that's exactly what God wants!

To find golden words, use the Golden Rule: when choosing the right words to say to someone else, think about the words that you would want to hear if you were standing in their shoes.

WOW

A lot of people have gone further than they thought they could because someone else told them that they could.

Zig Ziglar

Express yourself: Your children desperately need to hear that you love them . . . from you! If you're bashful, shy, or naturally un-communicative, get over it.

Dear Lord,
if I choose my words carefully,
I can make people's lives better.
Today and every day, help me
choose the words that You want
me to speak so that I can help
others become the people
You want them to be.

Amen

7

Patience at Home

A foolish person loses his temper.
But a wise person controls his anger.

✻ ✻ ✻

Proverbs 29:11 ICB

Sometimes, it's easiest to become angry with the people we love most. After all, we know that they'll still love us no matter how angry we become. But even though it's easy to become angry at home, it's usually wrong.

The next time you're tempted to become angry with a brother or a sister or a parent, remember that these are the people who love you more than anybody else! Then, calm down. Peace is always beautiful, *especially* when it's peace at your house.

Speak respectfully to everybody, starting with parents, grandparents, teachers, and other adults . . . but don't stop there. Be respectful of all people, including yourself!

WOW
A person should live so that everybody knows he is a Christian, and most of all, his family ought to know.

D. L. Moody

Respectful behavior never goes out of style: Remember the good old days when children were supposed to be polite and respectful, especially to adults? For wise parents, those good old days are now.

Dear Lord,
make me respectful of all people,
and when I become angry with
my family and friends, let me be
quick to forgive and forget.
Let me be a patient, kind, loving
Christian today and always.

Amen

Let's Pray for Patience

8

Do not worry about anything. But pray
and ask God for everything you need.

❋ ❋ ❋

Philippians 4:6 ICB

Would you like to become a more patient person? Pray about it. Is there a person you don't like? Pray for a forgiving heart. Do you lose your temper more than you should? Ask God for help.

Whatever you need, ask God to help you. And, as you pray more, you'll discover that God is always near and that He's always ready to hear from you. So don't worry about things; pray about them. God is waiting . . . and listening!

Lots of prayers every day: of course you should pray at mealtime and bedtime, but that's just the beginning. You can offer lots of prayers to God all day long . . . and you should!

WOW

Always be happy. Never stop praying.
Give thanks whatever happens.
That is what God wants for you
in Christ Jesus.
1 Thessalonians 5:16-18 ICB

Make yours a house of prayer: Prayer changes things *and* it changes families. Make certain that it changes *yours*.

Dear Lord,
You are always near; let me
talk with You often. When I am
impatient, let me turn to You.
And, let me use prayer to find
the peace that You desire for
my life today and every day.

Amen

Being Patient and Kind to Everybody

I tell you the truth, whatever you did for one of the least of these brothers of mine, you did for me.

❀ ❀ ❀

Matthew 25:40 NIV

The Bible tells us that we should be patient with *everybody*, not just with parents, teachers, and friends. In the eyes of God, all people are *very* important, so we should treat them that way.

Of course it's easy to be nice to the people whom we want to impress, but what about everybody else? Jesus gave us clear instructions: He said that when we do a good deed for someone less fortunate than we are, we have also done a good deed for our Savior. And as Christians, that's *exactly* what we are supposed to do!

Everybody is a VIP: VIP means "Very Important Person." To God, everybody is a VIP, and we should treat every person with dignity, patience, and respect.

WOW

If we have the true love of God in our
hearts, we will show it in our lives.
We will not have to go up and down
the earth announcing it. We will show it
in everything we say or do.

D. L. Moody

Parent Tip

"The least of these . . . .": How did Jesus treat the people who lived on the edges of society? With patience, respect, and love. Hopefully, all of our children will see that same behavior reflected in the actions of their parents.

Dear Lord,
help me to be patient with
everyone I meet. Help me to be
respectful of all people, and help
me to say kind words and do
good deeds, today and every day.

Amen

Patience Is...

Always be humble and gentle. Be patient
and accept each other with love.

❀ ❀ ❀

Ephesians 4:2 ICB

The dictionary defines the word "patience" as "the ability to be calm, tolerant, and understanding." Here's what that means: the word "calm" means being in control of your emotions (not letting your emotions control you). The word "tolerant" means being kind and considerate to people who are different from you. And, the word "understanding" means being able to put yourself in another person's shoes.

If you can be calm, tolerant, and understanding, you will be the kind of person whose good deeds are a blessing to your family and friends. They will appreciate your good deeds, and so will God.

Make up your own definition: decide what the word "patience" means to you. Talk about that definition with your parents, and ask them for their ideas, too.

WOW

Patience means waiting for God faithfully, hopefully, and prayerfully. But patience also means being willing to accept God's timetable, not your own.

Marie T. Freeman

The best way to teach patience is to demonstrate it: Our actions speak so loudly that they usually drown out our words.

Dear Lord,
sometimes it's hard to be
a patient person, and that's
exactly when I should try my
hardest to be patient. Help me
to follow Your commandments by
being a patient, loving Christian,
even when it's hard.

Amen

11

Brothers and Sisters (and Cousins)

Show respect for all people. Love the brothers and sisters of God's family.

❀ ❀ ❀

1 Peter 2:17

How easy is it to become angry with our brothers and our sisters? Sometimes, *very* easy! It's silly, but it's true: sometimes we can become angry with the very people we love the most.

The Bible tells us to be patient with everybody, and that most certainly includes brothers and sisters (if we're lucky enough to have them). We must also be patient and kind to our cousins and friends. Why? Because it's the right thing to do, and because it's God's commandment. Enough said!

Say it! If you love your brother or sister (and, of course, you do!) say so. But don't stop there: let *all* your family members know that you love them . . . a lot!

WOW
The first essential for
a happy home is love.
Billy Graham

Be imaginative: There are so many ways to say, "I love you." Find them. Put love notes in lunch pails and on pillows; hug relentlessly; laugh, play, and pray with abandon. Remember that love is highly contagious, and that your task, as a parent, is to ensure that your children catch it.

Dear Lord,
let me be respectful of all
people, starting with my family
and friends. And, let me share
the love that I feel in my heart
with them . . . and with You!

Amen

12

A Loving Heart Goes a Long Way!

So these three things continue forever:
faith, hope, and love. And the greatest
of these is love.

✿ ✿ ✿

1 Corinthians 13:13 ICB

The words of 1 Corinthians 13:13 remind us that love is God's commandment: "But now abide faith, hope, love, these three; but the greatest of these is love" (v. 13 NASB). Faith is important, of course. So is hope. But, love is more important still.

Christ loved us first, and, as Christians, we are called upon to return His love by sharing it. Today, let's share Christ's love with our families and friends. When we do, we'll discover that a loving heart is also a patient heart. And, we'll discover that the more we love, the more patient we become.

Pray for a heart that is loving and patient, and remember that God answers prayer!

WOW
He who is filled with love is filled
with God Himself.

Saint Augustine

Getting enough sleep? If you find yourself short on patience, perhaps you're also short on sleep. If so, turn off the TV and go to bed. As your energy returns, so will your patience.

Dear Lord,
give me a heart that is filled
with love, patience, and concern
for others. Slow me down and
calm me down so that I can see
the needs of other people. And
then, give me a loving heart so
that I will do something about
the needs that I see.

Amen

13

How Patient Would Jesus Be?

A new command I give you:
Love one another. As I have loved you,
so you must love one another. By this
all men will know you are my disciples,
if you love one another.

❋ ❋ ❋

John 13:34-35 NIV

If you've lost patience with someone, or if you're angry, take a deep breath and then ask yourself a simple question: "How would Jesus behave if He were here?" The answer to that question will tell you what to do.

Jesus was quick to speak kind words, and He was quick to forgive others. We must do our best to be like Him. When we do, we will be patient, loving, understanding, and kind.

KiD TiP

When in doubt: do the thing that you think Jesus would do. And, of course, don't do something if you think that He wouldn't do it.

WOW

The crucial question for each of us is this: What do you think of Jesus, and do you yet have a personal acquaintance with Him?

Hannah Whitall Smith

Parent Tip

It starts with parents: Our children will learn about Jesus at church and, in some cases, at school. But, the ultimate responsibility for religious teachings should never be delegated to institutions outside the home. As parents, *we* must teach our children about the love and grace of Jesus Christ by our words *and* by our actions.

Dear Lord,
let me use Jesus as my guide for living. When I have questions about what to do or how to act, let me behave as He behaved. When I do so, I will be patient, loving, and kind, not just today, but every day that I live.

Amen

14

If at First You Don't Succeed ...

But the people who trust in the Lord will become strong again. They will rise up as an eagle in the sky. They will run without needing rest. They will walk without becoming tired.

❋❋❋

Isaiah 40:31 ICB

Perhaps you've tried to become a more patient person, but you're still falling back into your old habits. If so, don't be discouraged. Instead, be even more determined to become the person God wants you to be.

If you trust God, and if you keep asking Him to help you change bad habits, He will help you make yourself into a new person. So, if at first you don't succeed, keep praying. God is listening, and He's ready to help you become a better person *if* you ask Him . . . so ask Him!

Forgive . . . and then forgive some more!
Sometimes, you may forgive someone once
and then, at a later time, you may become
angry at that very same person again. If so,
you must forgive that person again . . . and
again . . . until your forgiveness is complete
and final.

WOW

A Christian is never in a state of
completion but always in the process
of becoming.

Martin Luther

Wait patiently for your child to grow up.
Some bad habits, like impulsive behaviors and
temper tantrums, are simply a sign of youth-
ful immaturity. If you maintain a steady hand,
a loving heart, and a level head, the bad behavior will, in all likelihood, subside as your
child matures.

71

Dear Lord,
help me to become a person
whose habits are pleasing to You.
Help me to change my bad habits
so that nothing can interfere
with my love for others or with
my love for You.

Amen

When Things Go
Wrong

15

Be patient when trouble comes.
Pray at all times.

✿✿✿

Romans 12:12 ICB

From time to time, all of us have to face troubles and disappointments. When we do, God stands ready to protect us. Psalm 147 promises, "He heals the brokenhearted" (v. 3 NIV), but it doesn't say that He heals them instantly. Usually, it takes time for God to heal His children.

If you find yourself in any kind of trouble, pray about it and ask God for help. And then be patient. God will work things out, just as He has promised, but He will do it in His own time and according to His own plan.

You can make it right . . . if you think you can! If you've made a mistake, apologize. If you've broken something, fix it. If you've hurt someone's feelings, apologize. If you failed at something, try again. There is *always* something you can do to make things better . . . so do it!

WOW
If God sends us on stony paths,
he provides strong shoes.
Corrie ten Boom

Be a booster, not a cynic: Even when our children make mistakes, we must not lose faith in them. Cynicism is contagious, and so is optimism. As parents, we must think and act accordingly.

Dear Lord,
sometimes life is so hard, but
with You, there is always hope.
Keep me mindful that there
is nothing that will happen
today that You and I can't
handle together.

Amen

16

There's a Time for Everything

To every thing there is a season, and
a time to every purpose under the heaven.

✤ ✤ ✤

Ecclesiastes 3:1 KJV

We human beings can be *so* impatient. We know what we want, and we know exactly when we want it: RIGHT NOW! But, God knows better. He has created a world that unfolds according to His own time-table, not ours.

As Christians, we must be patient as we wait for God to show us the wonderful plans that He has in store for us. And while we're waiting for God to make His plans clear, let's keep praying and keep giving thanks to the One who has given us more blessings than we can count.

Big, bigger, and *very* big plans. God has very big plans in store for your life, so trust Him and wait patiently for those plans to unfold. And remember: God's timing is best.

WOW

The stops of a good man are ordered by the Lord as well as his steps.

George Mueller

Sometimes, the answer to prayer is "No." God doesn't grant all of our requests, nor should He. We must help our children understand that our prayers are answered by a sovereign, all-knowing God, and that we must trust His answers.

Dear Lord,
sometimes I become impatient
for things to happen. Sometimes,
I want the world to unfold
according to my plan, not Yours.
Help me to remember, Lord, that
Your plan is best for me, not just
for today, but for all eternity.

Amen

When **17** I'm Angry

A person who does not quickly get angry
shows that he has understanding. But
a person who quickly loses his temper
shows his foolishness.

❋ ❋ ❋

Proverbs 14:29 ICB

When you're angry, you will be tempted to say things and do things that you'll regret later. But don't do them! Instead of doing things in a hurry, slow down long enough to calm yourself down.

Jesus does not intend that you strike out against other people, and He doesn't intend that your heart be troubled by anger. Your heart should instead be filled with love, just like Jesus' heart was . . . and is!

Time out! If you become angry, the time to step away from the situation is *before* you say unkind words or do unkind things—not after. It's perfectly okay to place *yourself* in "time out" until you can calm down.

WOW
Bitterness and anger, usually over trivial things, make havoc of homes, churches, and friendships.

Warren Wiersbe

Parent Tip

Don't fan the flames: When your children become angry or upset, you'll tend to become angry and upset, too. Resist that temptation. As the grown-up person in the family, it's up to you to remain calm, even when other, less mature members of the family can't.

Dear Lord,
help me not to be an angry
person, but instead, make me a
forgiving person. Help me to
forget past disappointments
and to forgive those who have
disappointed me. Fill my heart
not with bitterness, but with
love for others . . . and for You.

Amen

18
Stop and Think

A wise person's mind tells him what to say.

❋ ❋ ❋

Proverbs 16:23 ICB

When we lose control of our emotions, we do things that we shouldn't do. Sometimes, we throw tantrums. How silly! Other times we pout or whine. Too bad!

The Bible tells us that it is foolish to become angry and that it is wise to remain calm. That's why we should learn to slow down and to think about things before we do them.

Do you want to make life better for yourself and for your family? Then be patient and think things through. Stop and think before you do things, not after. It's the wise thing to do.

Temper tantrums? No way! If you think you might lose your temper, stop and catch your breath, and walk away if you must. It's better to walk away than it is to let your temper control you.

WOW

When you strike out in anger, you may miss the other person, but you will always hit yourself.

Jim Gallery

When you lose your temper or make a mistake, apologize: No parent is perfect, not even you. Consequently, you will make mistakes from time to time (and yes, you might even lose your temper). When you do, apologize to the offended party, especially if that party is related to you by birth.

Dear Lord,
I can be *so* impatient, and I can become *so* angry. Calm me down, Lord, and make me a patient, forgiving Christian, today and every day of my life.

Amen

19

A Patient Heart

My dear brothers, always be willing to
listen and slow to speak. Do not become
angry easily. Anger will not help you live
a good life as God wants.

❋ ❋ ❋

James 1:19 ICB

In the Book of James, we learn that God has a "good life" that He wants each of us to live. But if we lose patience and become angry with others, our own anger can interfere with God's plans.

Do you want the good life that God has planned for you? If so, don't let your own anger get in the way. In other words, don't interfere with your own happiness. Instead, calm down and get ready for the wonderful life that God has promised to those whose hearts are filled with patience and with love.

Think carefully . . . make that *very* carefully! If you're a little angry, think carefully before you speak. If you're very angry, think *very* carefully. Otherwise, you might say something in anger that you would regret later.

WOW
Patience is the companion of wisdom.
Saint Augustine

Wise role models are a good thing to have: If you can control your anger, you'll help your children see the wisdom in controlling theirs.

Dear Lord,
sometimes, in moments of
frustration, I become angry.
When I do, remind me that
I must be understanding and
patient with others. Give me
a patient heart, Lord, and let
others see Your love reflected
through the things that I say
and the things that I do.

Amen

20

Solomon Says

Foolish people are always getting into quarrels, but avoiding quarrels will bring you honor.

✿ ✿ ✿

Proverbs 20:3 ICB

In Proverbs King Solomon gave us wonderful advice for living wisely. Solomon warned that impatience and anger lead only to trouble. And he was right!

The next time you're tempted to say an unkind word or to start an argument, remember Solomon. He was one of the wisest men who ever lived, and he knew that it's always better to be patient. So remain calm, and remember that patience is best. After all, if it's good enough for a wise man like Solomon, it should be good enough for you, too.

Tempted to fight? Walk away. The best fights are those that never happen.

WOW
Some fights are lost even though we win.
Vance Havner

Don't give fighting a fighting chance. When we grownups fight, our fights can have very grownup consequences. If we are to be positive role models for our children, we must *stand* on principle, but we must also *walk away* from violence.

Dear Lord,
when I become angry,
help me to remember that
You offer me peace. Let me turn
to You for wisdom, for patience,
and for the peace that
only You can give.

Amen

21
Listening to God

The thing you should want most is God's
kingdom and doing what God wants.
Then all these other things you need
will be given to you.

❀ ❀ ❀

Matthew 6:33 ICB

God has a perfect idea of the kind of people He wants us to become. And for starters, He wants us to be loving, kind, and patient—not rude or mean!

The Bible tells us that God is love and that if we wish to know Him, we must have love in our hearts. Sometimes, of course, when we're tired, angry, or frustrated, it is very hard for us to be loving. Thankfully, anger and frustration are feelings that come and go, but God's love lasts forever.

If you'd like to become a more patient person, talk to God in prayer, listen to what He says, and share His love with your family and friends. God is always listening, and He's ready to talk to you . . . now!

Quiet please! This world is LOUD! To hear what God has to say, you'll need to turn down the music and turn off the television long enough for God to get His message through.

WOW

An essential condition of listening to God is that the mind should not be distracted by thoughts of resentment, anger, hatred or revenge.

R. V. G. Tasker

If silence is golden, reading is silver: how precious are the hours we spend reading *to* our children and *with* them. In those quiet moments, *they* are blessed, and so, of course, are *we*.

PRAY TiME

Dear Lord,
let me be a person who prays
often. Let me spend quiet
moments with You so that I can
see more clearly the way that
You want me to go, today and
every day that I live.

Amen

22

A Little More Patient Every Day

A foolish person loses his temper.
But a wise person controls his anger.

❈ ❈ ❈

Proverbs 29:11 ICB

Do you want to become a person who is perfectly patient? And would you like to become that person today? Sorry! You've got to be patient, even when it comes to becoming more patient!

It's impossible to grow up all at once. Instead, we must grow up a little each day. And that's the way it is with patience: we can become a little more patient each day, and we should try our best to do so. When we do, we grow up to become wise adults. And just think: we will have acquired all that wisdom one day at a time!

Be patient with others and with your-self: an important part of growing up is learning to be patient with others *and* with yourself. And one more thing: learn from everybody's mistakes, *especially your own.*

WOW
God loves us the way we are, but He loves us too much to leave us that way.
Leighton Ford

Be patient with your child's impatience: children are supposed to be more impulsive than adults; after all, they're still kids. So be understanding of your child's limitations and understanding of his imperfections.

Dear Lord,
let me become a little more
grown up every day. Let me
become the kind of person that
You want me to be, Lord, and
then let me keep growing up
every day that I live.

Amen

23

Words Are Important

Pleasant words are like a honeycomb.
They make a person happy and healthy.

✿ ✿ ✿

Proverbs 16:24 ICB

When we become angry, we may say things that are hurtful to other people. But when we strike out at others with the intention to hurt them, we are not doing God's will. God intends that His children treat others with patience, kindness, dignity, and respect. As Christians, we must do our best to obey our Creator.

Are you tempted to say an unkind word? Don't! Words are important, and once you say them, you can't call them back. But if you're wise, you won't need to!

Patience

Stop, think, then speak: If you want to make your words useful instead of hurtful, don't open your mouth until you've turned on your brain and given it time to warm up.

WOW

Words. Do we fully understand their power? Can any of us really grasp the mighty force behind the things we say? Do we stop and think before we speak, considering the power of the words we speak?

Joni Eareckson Tada

Parents set the tone: As parents, it's up to us to establish the general tone and content of the conversations that take place in our homes. Let's make certain that the words we speak are worthy of the One we worship.

Dear Lord,
make me a person of patience
and kindness. Make the things
that I say and do helpful to
others, so that through me,
they might see You.

Amen

24

What the Bible Says

Your word is like a lamp for my feet
and a light for my way.

❋ ❋ ❋

Psalm 119:105 ICB

*A*re you having trouble with your temper, or with anything else for that matter? The answer to your problems can be found in God's Holy Word: the Bible.

The Bible is God's instruction book for living. If you learn what the Bible says, and if you follow its instructions, you will be blessed now and forever. So get to know your Bible; it's never too soon to become an expert on God's Word.

Take care of your Bible! It's the most important book you own . . . by far!

WOW

The strength of our spiritual lives will be exactly equal to the place held by the Bible in our lives and in our thoughts.

George Mueller

Children's Bible? Take a close look. If your child doesn't already own one, consider purchasing a translation of the Holy Bible specifically intended for children. These translations are amazingly helpful because of their simplicity and clarity.

Dear Lord,
You have given me a marvelous
gift: the Holy Bible. Let me
read it and understand it
and believe it and follow the
commandments that I find
there—every day that I live.

Amen

25

Patience With Parents

Honor your father and your mother.

❀ ❀ ❀

Exodus 20:25 ICB

Nobody's perfect, not even your parents. So the next time you're tempted to become angry with mom or dad for something they did or didn't do, stop and think about how much your parents do for you.

Sometimes, it's hard being a kid; that's for sure. But it can also be hard being a parent. Being a parent is a job with plenty of work to do, plenty of responsibilities to shoulder, and plenty of decisions to make. And if your parents make a bad decision every now and then, that's to be expected. So be patient with your parents . . . *very* patient. They've earned it.

Kid Tip

Calm down . . . sooner rather than later! If you're angry with your mom or your dad, don't blurt out something unkind. If you can't say anything nice, go to your room and don't come out until you can.

WOW
Whoever brings trouble with his family will be left with nothing but the wind.
Proverbs 11:29 ICB

Parent Tip

Hey Mom and Dad, how do you treat *your* parents? If you're lucky enough to have parents who are living, remember that the way you treat *them* is the way you're training your kids to treat *you*.

Dear Lord,
make me patient and
respectful toward my parents;
let me give them honor and love;
and let my behavior be pleasing
to them . . . and to You.

Amen

26

Need Help?
Ask God!

We pray that the Lord will lead
your hearts into God's love
and Christ's patience.

❋ ❋ ❋

2 Thessalonians 3:5 ICB

Do you need help in becoming a more patient person? If so, ask God; He's always ready, willing, and able to help. In fact, the Bible promises that when we sincerely seek God's help, He will give us the things we need.

So, if you want to become a better person, bow your head and start praying about it. And then rest assured that with God's help, you *can* change for the better . . . and you will!

Don't be too hard on yourself: you don't have to be perfect to be wonderful.

WOW

God will help us become the people we are meant to be, if only we will ask Him.

Hannah Whitall Smith

Don't be too hard on yourself, Part II: you don't have to be a perfect parent to be a godly one. Do the best you can, and leave the rest up to God.

Dear Lord,
I have so much to learn and so
many ways to improve myself,
but You love me just as I am.
Thank You for Your love and
for Your Son. And, help me to
become the person that
You want me to become.

Amen

27

Think First, Speak Later, Help Others!

A good person's words will help many others.

Proverbs 10:21 ICB

When we become frustrated or tired, it's easier to speak first and think second. But that's not the best way to talk to people. The Bible tells us that "a good person's words will help many others." But if our words are to be helpful, we must put some thought into them.

The next time you're tempted to say something unkind, remember that your words can and should be helpful to others, not hurtful. God wants to use you to make this world a better place, and He will use the things that you say to help accomplish that goal . . . *if* you let Him.

When talking to other people, ask your-self this question: "How helpful can I be?"

WOW
We should never be self-centered.
In our thoughts and prayers, we must try
to see the needs of others as clearly
as we see our own.

John Calvin

Encouragement 101: Take every opportun-ity to teach your children ways to encourage other people. And, while you're at it, make your own home an oasis of encouragement in a difficult world.

Dear Lord,
I want my words to help other
people. Let me choose my words
carefully so that when I speak,
the world is a better place
because of the things
I have said.

Amen

28

Peace is Beautiful!

I leave you peace. My peace I give you.
I do not give it to you as the world does.
So don't let your hearts be troubled.

✿ ✿ ✿

John 14:27 ICB

The beautiful words from John 14:27 remind us that Jesus offers us peace, not as the world gives, but as He alone gives. We, as believers, can accept His peace or ignore it. When we accept the peace of Jesus Christ into our hearts, our lives are changed forever, and we become more loving, patient Christians.

Christ's peace is offered freely; it has already been paid for; it is ours for the asking. So let us ask . . . and then share.

Count to ten . . . but don't stop there!:
If you're angry with someone, don't say the
first thing that comes to your mind. Instead,
catch your breath and start counting until
you are once again in control of your temper. If you count to a million and you're still
counting, go to bed! You'll feel better in the
morning.

WOW

Peace with God is where all peace begins.

Jim Gallery

Peace starts at home . . . and as the parent, you're in charge of keeping the peace.
It's a big job, so don't be afraid to ask for
help . . . especially God's help.

Dear Lord,
help me to accept Your peace
and then to share it with others,
today and forever.

Amen

29

Being a Patient Friend

A friend loves you all the time.
❈ ❈ ❈
Proverbs 17:17 ICB

Having friends requires patience. From time to time, even our most considerate friends may do things that make us angry. Why? Because they not perfect. Neither, of course, are we.

Today and every day, let us be understanding and patient with our friends. If we forgive them when *they* make mistakes, then perhaps they will forgive us when *we* make mistakes. And then, because we are patient and forgiving with each other, we will build friendships that will last.

If you're having trouble forgiving some-one else . . . think how many times other people have forgiven you!

WOW

Friendship is one of the sweetest
joys of life.

C. H. Spurgeon

Kids tend to behave like their friends behave: that's why it's important that you take your children to places where the friends they make are more likely to behave *as you want your children to behave* (church, of course, is one of those places).

Dear Lord,
let me be patient and
understanding toward my
friends. Lord, help me to
remember that we all make
mistakes and help me
to forgive my friends,
like You have forgiven me.

Amen

30

Growing Up!

And a servant of the Lord must not
quarrel! He must be kind to everyone.
He must be a good teacher.
He must be patient.

❋ ❋ ❋

2 Timothy 2:24 ICB

When do we stop growing up? Hopefully never! If we keep studying God's Word, and if we obey His commandments, we will never be "fully grown" Christians. We will always be growing.

God intends that we continue growing in the love and knowledge of Christ. And when we do so, we become more patient, more loving, more understanding, and more Christ-like. And we keep growing and growing . . . and growing!

Read the Bible? Every day!: try to read the Bible with your parents every day. If they forget, remind them!

WOW

Keep your face upturned to Christ as the flowers do to the sun. Look, and your soul shall live and grow.

Hannah Whitall Smith

Daily devotionals never go out of style: are you too busy to lead a daily devotional with your family? If so, it's time to reorder your priorities.

Dear Lord,
let me keep learning about Your
love and Your Son as long as I
live. Make me a better person
today than I was yesterday, but
not as good a person as I can
become tomorrow if I continue
to trust in You.

Amen

It Starts on the Inside and Works Its Way Out

31

God's holy people must be patient. They must obey God's commands and keep their faith in Jesus.

✿ ✿ ✿

Revelation 14:12 ICB

Where does patience start? It starts on the inside and works its way out. When our hearts are right with God, patience is a natural consequence of our love for Him.

Psalm 37:7 commands us to wait patiently for God, but, for most of us, waiting quietly for Him is difficult. Why? Because we are imperfect people who seek immediate answers to our problems. We don't like to wait for anybody or anything. But, God instructs us to be patient *in all things*, and that is as it should be. After all, think how patient God has been with us.

God and your parents have been patient with you . . . now it's your turn to be patient with others.

WOW
It is the duty of every Christian to be Christ to his neighbor.
Martin Luther

Don't be bothered by the minor inconveniences: life is far too short, and besides, your children are watching *and* learning . . . from you.

PRAY TiME

Dear Lord,
give me patience in matters both
great and small. You have been
patient with me, Lord; let me be
loving, patient, and kind to my
family and to my friends,
today and always.

Amen

Bible Verses to Memorize

I am come that
they might have life,
and that they might have it
more abundantly.

❋ ❋ ❋

John 10:10 KJV

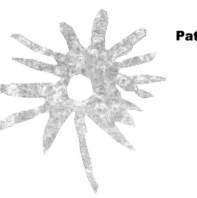

For ye have need of patience,
that, after ye have done
the will of God, ye might receive
the promise.

❀ ❀ ❀

Hebrews 10:36 KJV

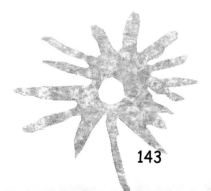

For when the way is rough,
your patience has a chance
to grow. So let it grow, and
don't try to squirm out of
your problems.

❀ ❀ ❀

James 1:3-4 TLB

Patience

The LORD is good to those
whose hope is in him,
to the one who seeks him;
it is good to wait quietly for
the salvation of the LORD.

❀ ❀ ❀

Lamentations 3:25-26 NIV

Wait on the LORD,
and he shall save thee.

❀ ❀ ❀

Proverbs 20:22 KJV

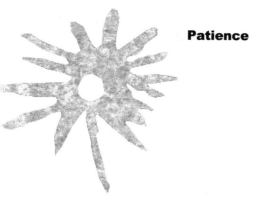

Patience

Don't be impatient for the LORD
to act! Travel steadily along
his path. He will honor you....

❋ ❋ ❋

Psalm 37:34 NLT

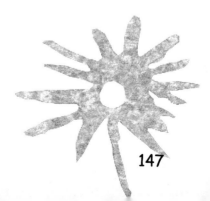

But the fruit of the Spirit
is love, joy, peace, patience,
kindness, goodness,
faithfulness. . . .

❁ ❁ ❁

Galatians 5:22 NASB

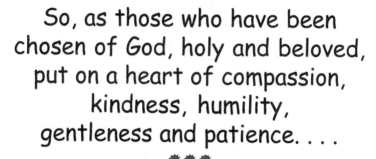

So, as those who have been
chosen of God, holy and beloved,
put on a heart of compassion,
kindness, humility,
gentleness and patience. . . .

❀ ❀ ❀

Colossians 3:12 NASB

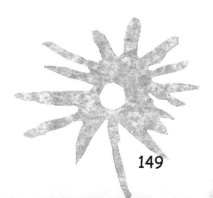

The end of a matter
is better than its beginning,
and patience is better
than pride.

❀ ❀ ❀

Ecclesiastes 7:8 NIV

Patience

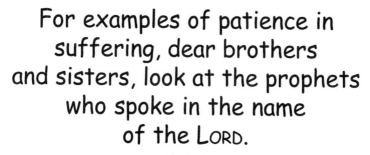

For examples of patience in
suffering, dear brothers
and sisters, look at the prophets
who spoke in the name
of the LORD.

❀ ❀ ❀

James 5:10 NLT

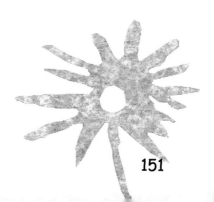

Be patient, then, brothers,
until the L O R D's coming.
See how the farmer waits
for the land to yield its
valuable crop and
how patient he is for
the autumn and spring rains.

❀ ❀ ❀

James 5:7 NIV

For God is pleased with you
when, for the sake of your
conscience, you patiently endure
unfair treatment.

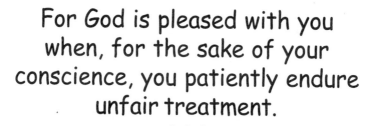

1 Peter 2:19 NLT

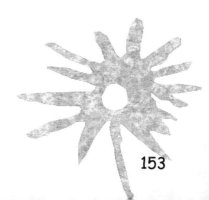

May God,
who gives this patience and
encouragement, help you live
in complete harmony with
each other—each with the
attitude of Christ Jesus
toward the other.

❋ ❋ ❋

Romans 15:5 NLT

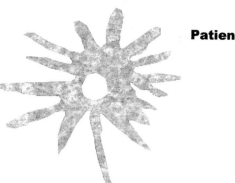

But if we hope for what we do not yet have, we wait for it patiently.

Romans 8:25 NIV

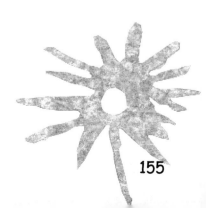

A man's wisdom gives
him patience; it is to his
glory to overlook an offense.

❋ ❋ ❋

Proverbs 19:11 NIV

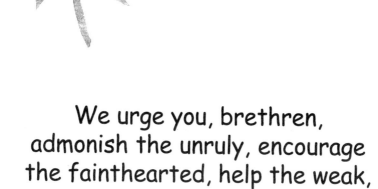

We urge you, brethren,
admonish the unruly, encourage
the fainthearted, help the weak,
be patient with everyone.

❀ ❀ ❀

1 Thessalonians 5:14 NASB

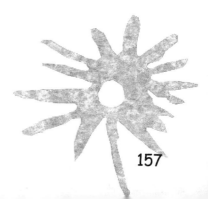

Little Book Devotions help parents and children discuss important Biblical themes by relating those themes to the challenges of everyday life. These books are intended to be read *by* parents *to* children. Current titles include:

Little Book Devotions Honesty
Little Book Devotions Kindness
Little Book Devotions Patience

Additional titles are coming soon.

Little Book Devotions are available in LifeWay Christian Stores.